D0787494

WILD BACKYARD ANIMALS

Watch Out for COYOTES!

Elaine McKinnon

PowerKiDS press.

New York

Published in 2016 by The Rosen Publishing Group, Inc.
29 East 21st Street, New York, NY 10010

Copyright © 2016 by The Rosen Publishing Group, Inc.

First Edition

Editor: Caitlin McAneney
Book Design: Katelyn Heinle

Photo Credits: Cover Geoffrey Kuchera/Shutterstock.com; back cover, pp. 3, 4, 6–8, 10, 12, 14, 16, 18–20, 22–24 (background) Polovinkin/Shutterstock.com; p. 5 Derek R. Audette/Shutterstock.com; p. 7 (map) Volina/Shutterstock.com; p. 7 (eastern coyote) Tom Reichner/Shutterstock.com; p. 7 (western coyote) robert cicchetti/Shutterstock.com; p. 9 kojihirano/Shutterstock.com; p. 10 Volt Collection/Shutterstock.com; p. 11 Randimal/Shutterstock.com; p. 12 Steve Winter/National Geographic/Getty Images; p. 13 Critterbiz/Shutterstock.com; p. 14 Josef Pittner/Shutterstock.com; p. 15 Kane513/Shutterstock.com; p. 17 Roberta Olenick/ All Canada Photos/Getty Images; p. 19 (family hiking) JaySi/Shutterstock.com; p. 19 (sign) Mark Williamson Stock Photography/ Stockbyte/Getty Images; p. 20 MarclSchauer/Shutterstock.com; p. 21 Julie Lubick/Shutterstock.com; p. 22 Betty Shelton/ Shutterstock.com.

Cataloging-in-Publication Data

McKinnon, Elaine.
Watch out for coyotes! / by Elaine McKinnon.
p. cm. — (Wild backyard animals)
Includes index.
ISBN 978-1-5081-4259-1 (pbk.)
ISBN 978-1-5081-4260-7 (6-pack)
ISBN 978-1-5081-4276-8 (library binding)
1. Coyote — Juvenile literature. I. McKinnon, Elaine. II. Title.
QL737.C22 M35 2016
599.77'25—d23

CONTENTS

A HAUNTING HOWL

Do you hear that **howl** in the night? It's the call of the coyote—a wild animal that doesn't always stay in the wild.

Coyotes are wild animals in the canine animal family, which includes wolves, foxes, and dogs. But these wild canines have **adapted** to nearly every **environment** in North America. It's not uncommon to spot a coyote as you walk in the woods or hike in the mountains. You might even find one in your backyard!

THERE ARE MANY NATIVE AMERICAN LEGENDS ABOUT A TRICKY AND CLEVER CHARACTER NAMED COYOTE.

4

WHERE DO COYOTES LIVE?

At one time, you would only have been able to find the coyote in a certain location. They lived in the western United States and Mexico. They preferred living in grasslands and deserts.

Many animals' populations have dropped since people widely settled across North America. However, the coyote **thrived**. It will eat almost anything—even trash! It began to settle outside its range. Today, you can find coyotes in grasslands, forests, mountains, and even backyards and cities across North America.

THERE ARE TWO KINDS OF COYOTES IN NORTH AMERICA—EASTERN COYOTES AND WESTERN COYOTES. THE EASTERN COYOTE IS FOUND IN THE NORTHEAST, WHILE THE WESTERN COYOTE IS FOUND FARTHER WEST.

U.S. (ALASKA)

CANADA

PACIFIC OCEAN

UNITED STATES

ATLANTIC OCEAN

MEXICO

COYOTE TERRITORY

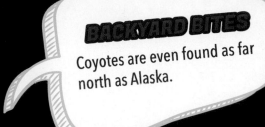

BACKYARD BITES

Coyotes are even found as far north as Alaska.

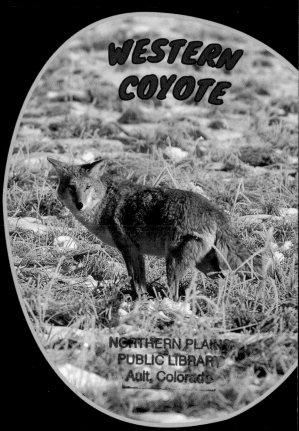

WESTERN COYOTE

NORTHERN PLAINS PUBLIC LIBRARY
Ault, Colorado

EASTERN COYOTE

7

IDENTIFYING A COYOTE

How can you identify a coyote? Coyotes look like midsized dogs with pointed ears. Their fur comes in different colors, but most are light brown with gray and black down their back. Their long tail has a black tip.

Coyotes' pointed ears help them listen for **prey**, predators, and the calls of other coyotes. They use a strong sense of smell to find food. They also have great eyesight.

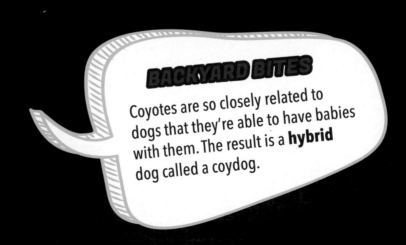

BACKYARD BITES

Coyotes are so closely related to dogs that they're able to have babies with them. The result is a **hybrid** dog called a coydog.

COYOTES GROW TO AROUND 3 FEET (0.9 M) LONG AND HAVE A TAIL THAT'S ABOUT 16 INCHES (41 CM) LONG.

AWESOME ADAPTATIONS

Coyotes were able to move out of their home range because they're adaptable. Unlike many animals, they're able to live in cold, wet **habitats** as well as hot and dry habitats. They live in groups called packs, which helps them find more food.

Coyotes are excellent hunters. They're not picky about food, so they'll eat anything they can kill or find. Plus, they can chase prey at speeds of up to 40 miles (64 km) an hour!

COYOTES ARE GREAT SWIMMERS. THEY CAN SWIM LONG DISTANCES FOR FOOD.

10

BACKYARD BITES

Another adaptation of coyotes is **camouflage**. The color of their fur makes it easy for them to hide in tall grass or trees.

A HUNTER AND A SCAVENGER

Coyotes are omnivores, which means they eat both plants and animals. They hunt and eat any animal they can catch—from bugs to deer. They enjoy rabbits, snakes, and mice, too. Sometimes coyotes dine on vegetables and fruit, such as cactus fruit and berries.

Coyotes are also scavengers, which means they'll eat whatever they can find. They'll eat the dead bodies of large animals, such as bison and elk. They'll even go through trash in your backyard.

BACKYARD BITES

Coyotes are usually nocturnal, which means they're most active at night. Nocturnal animals, including outdoor pets, should fear this hungry hunter!

12

COYOTES PLAY A BIG PART IN THEIR ECOSYSTEM AS PREDATORS.

13

FROM PUP TO PREDATOR

Coyote pups, or babies, are small and fluffy. Mother coyotes give birth to a litter of three to 12 pups in the springtime. Pups grow up in a den with both their mother and father taking care of them.

Coyote parents have to find extra food for their babies. They **protect** their babies from predators. They also have to teach their pups how to hunt. Within a few months, pups are ready to find their own food. Coyotes can live between 10 and 14 years in the wild.

BACKYARD BITES

Coyotes mate for life. That means a mother and father coyote stick together as long as they live.

COYOTES COMMUNICATE THROUGH HOWLS. THIS HELPS THEM FIND ONE ANOTHER AT THE END OF A HUNT.

15

COYOTE ATTACKS

Coyotes can cause major problems for people. Since they'll hunt and scavenge anything they can, they make messes out of trash. They'll also kill livestock on farms, such as baby sheep and cows.

Coyote attacks on people aren't common, but they do happen. It's most common around Los Angeles, California. Some coyotes are losing their fear of people because people are feeding them. Coyotes are more likely to attack small pets, such as cats and smaller dogs.

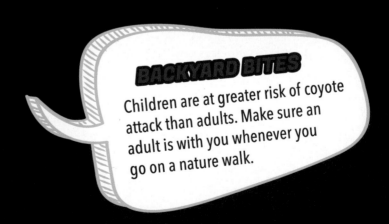

BACKYARD BITES

Children are at greater risk of coyote attack than adults. Make sure an adult is with you whenever you go on a nature walk.

COYOTES CAN CARRY RABIES. THEY CAN PASS THIS ILLNESS TO A PERSON OR OTHER ANIMAL THROUGH A BITE.

SAFETY TIPS

How can you stay safe from coyotes? First, never feed them. If you feed a coyote, it stops being afraid over time and starts expecting food.

If you see a coyote, try to make yourself look big and scary. Wave your arms and stand tall. Don't run away, or it might chase you. Make lots of noise by clapping, yelling, or using a noisemaker to scare it away. For your pets' safety, keep them inside at night. Keep them on a leash when you're walking.

BACKYARD BITES

Make sure your parents keep their garbage locked up and pet food inside. Coyotes will probably leave a neighborhood if there's nothing to eat.

18

IF YOU LIVE IN AN AREA KNOWN FOR COYOTES, BRING A NOISEMAKER WITH YOU ON WALKS. YOU CAN BUY AN AIR HORN THAT MAKES A LOUD SOUND. YOU CAN ALSO FILL A CAN WITH MARBLES TO SHAKE.

Do not feed the coyotes

19

COYOTE DANGERS

Coyote populations aren't in trouble right now. In fact, coyotes are still thriving. As they lose their wild habitat to new buildings, they adapt to neighborhoods and cities.

However, coyotes aren't completely safe. Predators of the coyote include larger animals, such as wolves, bears, and mountain lions. People are the greatest risk to coyotes, though. Many are killed and trapped for sport. Some farmers blame livestock deaths on coyotes and don't hesitate to kill them.

WOLF

BACKYARD BITES

In 1995, wolves were brought back to Yellowstone National Park, and they made the coyote population drop quickly.

20

MANY COYOTES ARE HIT BY CARS ON BUSY ROADS.

THE CLEVER COYOTE

The coyote is one animal that doesn't mind sneaking around. Even if you have a fence, a coyote can get in. Though they don't bite people often, it's good to know how to keep yourself and your pets safe.

These canines have many cool features, from their adaptability to their howls. They can find their way into cities and backyards, and they can sniff out a meal anywhere. Native American tales about the coyote are right—it's a very clever creature.

adapt: To change to fit new conditions.

camouflage: Colors or shapes on animals that allow them to blend in with their surroundings.

communicate: To share ideas and feelings through sounds and motions.

ecosystem: All the living things in an area.

environment: The natural world in which a plant or animal lives.

habitat: The natural home for plants, animals, and other living things.

howl: The long, loud cry of a wild animal, such as a wolf or dog.

hybrid: The offspring of two animals or plants of different kinds.

legend: A story handed down from the past.

prey: An animal hunted by other animals for food.

protect: To keep safe.

rabies: A deadly disease that affects the central nervous system. It is carried in the spit of some animals.

thrive: To grow successfully.

INDEX

A

attacks, 16

C

calls, 4, 8

camouflage, 11

D

dogs, 4, 8

E

ears, 8

eastern coyote, 6, 7

F

food, 8, 10, 14, 18

fur, 8, 11

H

habitats, 10, 20

howl, 4, 15, 22

hunters, 10, 12, 14, 15, 16

L

livestock, 16, 20

O

omnivores, 12

P

packs, 10

pets, 12, 16, 18, 22

predators, 8, 13, 14, 20

prey, 8, 10

pups, 14

R

rabies, 17

range, 6, 10

S

scavengers, 12, 16

T

tail, 8, 9

W

western coyote, 6, 7

wolves, 4, 20

WEBSITES

Due to the changing nature of Internet links, PowerKids Press has developed an online list of websites related to the subject of this book. This site is updated regularly. Please use this link to access the list: www.powerkidslinks.com/wba/coyo

24